# FIVE RULES FOR

# SUCCESSFUL

# BUSINESS EMAIL

# COMMUNICATION

## MAKSYM TANASOV

For more information, or to book an event, contact :

**author.m.tanasov@gmail.com**

Book design by  Maksym Tanasov

Cover design by Maksym Tanasov

ISBN - Paperback: 9798397410717

ISBN - Hardcover : 9798397411677

# CONTENTS

# Chapter 1

# Establishing a Professional Tone

## Understanding the importance of professionalism in business mail communication

In today's fast-paced digital era, mail has become an indispensable tool for business communication. As a highly qualified specialist in business and marketing, I am keenly aware of the paramount importance of professionalism in mail correspondence. Mastering the art of composing business mails not only demonstrates competence and expertise but also has the potential to elevate your reputation, strengthen relationships, and drive success in the corporate world. In this article, we will explore the profound significance of professionalism in business mail communication, providing insights and practical tips to help you navigate this essential aspect of modern business.

### Making a Positive First Impression:

The adage "first impressions matter" holds true, even in the realm of virtual communication. Your mail is often the first point of contact with clients, partners, or colleagues, and it sets the tone for future interactions. By adopting a professional approach, you convey reliability, credibility, and respect for the recipient's time and attention. Ensure your mails are free from typographical errors, use appropriate salutations, and maintain a courteous tone throughout. Remember, a well-crafted message is your gateway to building fruitful business relationships.

### Crafting Clear and Concise Messages:

The efficiency and effectiveness of business communication rely on clarity and conciseness. Professionalism demands that you express your ideas in a succinct manner, providing relevant information without overwhelming the recipient. Organize your thoughts logically, use bullet points or numbered lists when applicable, and adopt a structure that facilitates easy comprehension. By doing so, you enhance the readability of your mail, reduce the chances of misinterpretation, and showcase your professionalism through concise and actionable messages.

### Tailoring Tone and Language:

Understanding your audience is crucial when crafting business mails. Different recipients require different approaches, and adapting your tone and language accordingly is a hallmark of professional. While maintaining a respectful and formal tone is generally advisable, adjusting your communication style to match the recipient's preferences can foster rapport and build stronger connections. Pay attention to cultural nuances, avoid jargon, and strike a balance between being approachable and maintaining a professional demeanor.

### Timeliness and Efficiency:

In the fast-paced world of business, time is a precious commodity. Demonstrating professionalism in your mail correspondence entails prompt responses and efficient communication. Strive to reply to mails within a reasonable timeframe, even if it is to acknowledge receipt and inform the sender of the expected response time. Additionally, practice good mail etiquette by keeping your messages concise and to the point. Respect the recipient's time by avoiding unnecessary back-and-forth exchanges and provide all relevant information in a single mail. Such efficiency will not only portray your professionalism but also contribute to a seamless flow of communication.

## Maintaining Confidentiality and Security:

In the age of cyber threats and data breaches, maintaining confidentiality and security in business mail communication is paramount. Professional demands that you handle sensitive information responsibly, using encryption or secure channels whenever necessary. Take care to double-check recipients' mail addresses to prevent accidental data leakage, and avoid discussing confidential matters in unsecured environments. By prioritizing the protection of sensitive information, you establish trust and demonstrate your commitment to professional integrity.

# Choosing an appropriate salutation and closing

These seemingly simple components carry immense weight, setting the tone for your message and leaving a lasting impression on your recipients. In this article, we will delve into the art of selecting appropriate greetings and endings, exploring strategies to captivate your readers, foster connections, and make your business mails shine with competence and flair.

### Crafting Memorable Greetings:

The opening of an mail is your gateway to capturing the attention and interest of your recipients. An effective greeting should be courteous, personalized, and aligned with the nature of your professional relationship. While "Dear [Recipient's Name]" remains a classic choice for formal communication, consider tailoring your salutation based on your familiarity with the recipient. For closer relationships, a warmer greeting like "Hello [Recipient's Name]" or "Hi [Recipient's Name]" can infuse a touch of friendliness without compromising professionalism. By selecting an appropriate and engaging greeting, you set the stage for a positive and productive exchange.

### The Art of Sign-Offs:

The ending of your mail is equally significant, as it provides a memorable conclusion to your message and leaves a lasting impression. Your sign-off should reflect the tone of your communication, convey gratitude or appreciation, and reinforce professionalism. Traditional options like "Sincerely" or "Regards" are safe choices for formal or professional relationships. For a touch of warmth, consider "Best regards" or "Kind regards." Alternatively, you can experiment with less conventional but still professional options such as "Yours faithfully" or "Respectfully yours." Remember, your sign-off is your final opportunity to solidify your professionalism and leave a lasting positive impression.

### Tailoring to the Recipient:

Personalization is a powerful tool in business mail communication. By tailoring your greetings and endings to individual recipients, you demonstrate attentiveness and respect for their preferences. Take the time to learn about the cultural norms and communication styles of your recipients, and adjust your salutations and sign-offs accordingly. For instance, if you are corresponding with someone from a culture that values formalities, opt for a more traditional greeting and ending. Similarly, if you have an established rapport with a recipient, feel free to incorporate a more informal or friendly sign-off. Adapting to the preferences of your recipients showcases your professionalism and fosters stronger connections.

### Injecting Enthusiasm:

While professional is essential, there is room to infuse your greetings and endings with a touch of enthusiasm. Showcasing genuine interest and excitement can make your mails more engaging and memorable. Consider starting your mail with a warm "Good morning" or "Hope this mail finds you well." For the ending, you can express anticipation by using phrases like "Looking forward to your response" or "Excited to hear your thoughts." By demonstrating enthusiasm, you create an inviting atmosphere that encourages recipients to respond and fosters a positive impression of your professional.

### Adapting to the Context:

It is crucial to consider the context of your mail when selecting greetings and endings. If you are writing to a group or team, a collective greeting like "Hello everyone" or "Dear team" is appropriate. Similarly, if you are communicating with a senior executive, a more formal and respectful greeting is recommended. Pay attention to the nature of your relationship, the purpose of your mail, and the corporate culture to ensure your greetings and endings are aligned with the context. Adapting to specific circumstances demonstrates your keen awareness and professional.

# Using a clear and concise subject line

In today's fast-paced digital landscape, a clear and concise subject line can mean the difference between immediate engagement or getting lost in the ever-growing sea of unread mails. In this article, we will explore the art of crafting subject lines that command attention, provoke curiosity, and propel your mail communication to new heights of professional and effectiveness.

## Grabbing Attention with Brevity:

In the age of overflowing inboxes, brevity is a prized asset. The subject line acts as your mail's first impression, and a concise and attention-grabbing opener is crucial. Keep your subject line short and sweet, aiming for no more than 5 to 8 words. By concisely delivering your message, you ensure that your recipient's attention is immediately captured amidst the avalanche of mails they receive daily. Embrace brevity to make a lasting impact and entice your reader to open your mail.

## Conveying Relevance and Purpose:

The clarity in subject lines is paramount. Avoid vague or generic phrases that leave recipients guessing about the content of your mail. Instead, clearly state the purpose or topic of your message in a way that resonates with your audience. Use keywords that directly relate to the subject matter and prioritize essential information. For example, instead of a subject line like "Meeting," try "Request for Meeting: Project Update Needed." By conveying relevance and purpose upfront, you demonstrate professionalism and respect for your recipient's time.

### Evoking Curiosity and Intrigue:

While clarity is crucial, incorporating an element of curiosity or intrigue can pique the recipient's interest and increase the likelihood of your mail being opened. Consider using subject lines that tease valuable information, pose thought-provoking questions, or highlight exclusive opportunities. For instance, instead of a straightforward subject line like "Sales Report," you could write "Unlocking Hidden Revenue Streams: Insights from the Latest Sales Report." By striking a balance between clarity and curiosity, you stimulate engagement and set yourself apart in a sea of mundane mails.

### Leveraging Urgency and Action:

Subject lines that evoke a sense of urgency or imply a call to action can compel recipients to prioritize your mail. Incorporate time-sensitive words or phrases that create a sense of immediacy. For instance, "Deadline Approaching: Response Required by [Date]" or "Limited-Time Offer: Act Now to Secure Exclusive Benefits." However, use urgency sparingly and ensure that it aligns with the genuine urgency of the situation. By leveraging urgency and action in your subject lines, you motivate prompt responses and reinforce your professionalism as someone who respects deadlines and prioritizes efficiency.

### Testing and Optimizing for Effectiveness:

To maximize the impact of your subject lines, it is essential to test and optimize them over time. Experiment with different approaches, analyze open rates and learn from the results. A/B testing can be a valuable tool, allowing you to compare the effectiveness of various subject lines within your target audience. Pay attention to metrics and feedback, and continuously refine your approach to align with the preferences and behaviors of your recipients. By embracing a data-driven mindset, you can unlock the true potential of your subject lines and achieve optimal results.

# Avoiding slang, jargon, and unnecessary abbreviations

Business letters serve as powerful tools for conveying ideas, building relationships, and driving success. To ensure effective communication, it is vital to steer clear of slang, jargon, and unnecessary abbreviations that can hinder understanding and undermine your professionalism. In this article, we will explore the art of crafting business letters that exude clarity, resonate with your audience, and elevate your communication skills to new heights.

**Embrace Simplicity and Clarity:**

In the realm of business communication, simplicity and clarity reign supreme. Avoid the use of slang or colloquial expressions that may be unfamiliar to your recipients. Stick to straightforward and universally understood language to ensure your message is clear and easily comprehensible. Instead of relying on trendy or informal terms, choose words that convey your ideas concisely and accurately. By embracing simplicity, you demonstrate professionalism and eliminate the risk of miscommunication.

**Banish Jargon from Your Vocabulary:**

Jargon, the specialized language of a particular profession or industry, can be a barrier to effective communication. While it may be tempting to showcase your expertise through industry-specific terms, excessive use of jargon can alienate your readers who may not be familiar with the terminology. Opt for plain language that conveys your message without sacrificing clarity. If the use of technical terms is unavoidable, provide brief and clear explanations to ensure your recipients can follow along. By eliminating jargon, you bridge the gap between experts and non-experts, fostering better understanding and stronger connections.

**Opt for Complete Words over Abbreviations:**

Abbreviations, while convenient, can be a source of confusion and ambiguity. To maintain clarity and professional in your business letters, opt for complete words instead of relying on abbreviations. While some abbreviations may be widely recognized and accepted in your field, it is best to err on the side of caution. Spell out acronyms on their first mention, followed by the abbreviation in parentheses. This approach ensures that all recipients, including those unfamiliar with the abbreviations, can fully grasp your intended meaning. By using complete words, you avoid potential misunderstandings and showcase your commitment to clear and precise communication.

**Consider the Audience:**

Tailoring your language to your specific audience is vital in business letter writing. Take into account the knowledge, experience, and background of your recipients. If you are corresponding with individuals outside your field or clients who may not be well-versed in technical terms, adjust your language accordingly. Adopting a reader-centric approach shows respect for your audience and demonstrates your ability to communicate effectively across diverse backgrounds. By considering the audience, you position yourself as a professional who values clear and inclusive communication.

### Proofread and Edit Diligently:

Proofreading and editing are critical steps in ensuring your business letters are free from slang, jargon, and unnecessary abbreviations. Take the time to review your correspondence meticulously, checking for any instances of informal language or unclear abbreviations. Consider seeking a second pair of eyes to provide valuable feedback and identify potential pitfalls. By dedicating yourself to thorough proofreading and editing, you showcase your attention to detail and commitment to delivering polished and professional business letters.

# Maintaining a polite and respectful tone throughout the mail

Politeness and respect form the bedrock of professional relationships, fostering trust, cooperation, and long-term success. We will explore the art of crafting business letters that emanate politeness and respect, enabling you to establish rapport, convey professional, and leave a lasting positive impression on your recipients.

## Start with a Courteous Salutation:

The opening salutation of your letter sets the tone for the entire correspondence. Begin with a respectful and appropriate greeting, such as "Dear [Recipient's Name]" for formal communications or "Hello [Recipient's Name]" for more informal ones. This small gesture demonstrates your recognition of the recipient as an individual worthy of courtesy and respect. By initiating the letter with a polite salutation, you establish a foundation of professional and create a favorable impression.

## Use Polite and Diplomatic Language:

Throughout your letter, strive to use polite and diplomatic language that maintains a respectful tone. Be mindful of your choice of words, avoiding harsh or confrontational language that may damage relationships or undermine the purpose of your communication. Use phrases such as "I would like to kindly request," "I appreciate your attention to this matter," or "Thank you for your consideration." Such language conveys politeness, acknowledges the recipient's value, and fosters a positive atmosphere for productive dialogue.

### Employ Active Listening and Empathy:

Effective communication is not just about transmitting information; it also involves active listening and demonstrating empathy toward your recipients. Show genuine interest in their perspectives, needs, and concerns. Acknowledge their input and respond thoughtfully, even when delivering difficult messages. Employing active listening and empathy in your letter shows respect for the recipient's thoughts and feelings, nurturing a collaborative and respectful relationship.

### Maintain Professionalism in Conflict Resolution:

In business, conflicts can arise, and addressing them with a polite and respectful tone is essential for effective resolution. When discussing disagreements or addressing concerns, remain calm, objective, and focused on finding common ground. Avoid personal attacks or inflammatory language. Instead, present your points clearly and logically, using phrases like "I understand your perspective," "Let's work together to find a solution," or "I appreciate your patience in resolving this matter." By maintaining professionalism in conflict resolution, you preserve relationships and pave the way for constructive dialogue.

### Conclude with Gratitude and Respect:

As you bring your letter to a close, express gratitude and respect towards the recipient. Use courteous sign-offs such as "Sincerely," "Thank you for your time," or "Respectfully." Reinforce your appreciation for their attention, input, or assistance. This final gesture leaves a positive lasting impression and reinforces the respectful tone that permeates your entire letter.

# Chapter 2

# Writing Clear and Concise Messages

## Structuring mails effectively with a clear introduction, body, and conclusion

mails serve as powerful tools for communication, enabling us to connect with clients, colleagues, and stakeholders in a fast-paced digital world. We will delve into the art of crafting mails with a clear introduction, body, and conclusion, allowing you to create compelling and impactful communications that yield positive outcomes.

### Introduction: Captivating Attention from the Start

The introduction sets the stage for your mail and should be crafted to captivate the recipient's attention. Start with a polite greeting and a concise opening sentence that conveys the purpose or main point of your mail. Consider using a personal touch or referencing a recent interaction to establish rapport. A compelling introduction sets the tone for the rest of your mail, ensuring that your recipient is engaged and eager to continue reading.

### Body: Clear and Organized Delivery of Information

The body of your mail is where you provide the main content, supporting details, or requests. Structure the body in a logical and organized manner to ensure clarity and coherence. Break your information into paragraphs or bullet points for easy readability. Use clear and concise language to convey your message effectively. When presenting multiple points or discussing complex ideas, consider using headings or subheadings to guide your recipient through the content. By structuring the body effectively, you facilitate comprehension and make it easier for your recipient to navigate the information provided.

## Conclusion: Closing with a Clear Call to Action

The conclusion of your mail is your opportunity to guide the recipient toward a specific action or response. Summarize the key points discussed in the body and reiterate the main objective of your mail. Use a polite and assertive tone to clearly state your desired outcome or request. If appropriate, provide a deadline or specify the next steps. This concise conclusion helps the recipient understand the purpose of your mail and motivates them to take the desired action.

## Effective Use of Signatures and Closings

In addition to the structure of the mail itself, the proper use of signatures and closings is crucial to maintain professionalism and providing necessary contact information. Include a clear and professional mail signature that includes your name, job title, and contact details. Choose a closing that is appropriate for the context and relationship, such as "Sincerely," "Best regards," or "Thank you." This final touch adds a personal touch and reinforces your professional's.

# Keeping mails concise and to the point

In today's fast-paced world, attention spans are short, and time is precious. Crafting concise and to-the-point mails is crucial for capturing attention, conveying information effectively, and inspiring prompt action. We will explore strategies to keep your mails short and impactful, enabling you to make a lasting impression and achieve your communication goals efficiently.

### Start with a Clear Objective:

Before drafting your mail, define the objective you want to achieve. This clarity will guide you in selecting only the most essential information to include. Focus on a single topic or purpose to avoid overwhelming your recipient with unnecessary details. By starting with a clear objective, you set the foundation for a concise and purpose-driven mail.

### Use Clear and Direct Language:

When composing your mail, prioritize clarity and directness in your language. Be concise and avoid unnecessary verbosity or flowery language. Use short sentences and bullet points to convey your message efficiently. Stick to the main points, omitting irrelevant or tangential information. By using clear and direct language, you ensure that your message is easily understood and quickly absorbed.

### Prioritize Key Information:

Identify the most important information and place it prominently within your mail. Put yourself in the recipient's shoes and consider what they need to know upfront. If there are action items or specific requests, highlight them. Avoid burying essential details within lengthy paragraphs. By prioritizing key information, you ensure that your main points are immediately visible and increase the likelihood of your recipient taking the desired action promptly.

### Be Mindful of mail Length:

While there is no strict rule for mail length, being mindful of brevity is essential. Ideally, aim for mails that can be read and understood in a matter of minutes. If your mail extends beyond a few paragraphs, reassess its content and determine if all the information is necessary. Consider if any details can be moved to attachments or discussed in a separate conversation. By keeping your mail concise, you respect your recipient's time and increase the likelihood of a prompt response.

### Edit and Condense:

Once you've drafted your mail, take the time to edit and condense the content further. Eliminate redundant phrases or repetitive information. Consolidate multiple points into concise sentences. Remove any unnecessary filler words or phrases. Challenge yourself to convey the same message with fewer words. By diligently editing and condensing your mail, you sharpen your communication skills and maximize the impact of your message.

# Using bullet points, numbered lists, or subheadings to enhance readability

In today's fast-paced world, capturing and maintaining the attention of your readers is paramount. By leveraging the power of bullets, numbered lists, and subheadings, you can enhance the readability of your content, making it easier for your audience to absorb information and grasp key points. We will explore how these formatting tools can transform your business communication, captivating readers and driving meaningful engagement.

### Bullets: Simplifying Complex Ideas

Bullets are an invaluable tool for presenting information concisely and simplifying complex ideas. Use bullets to highlight key points or to present a list of items in a visually appealing manner. By breaking down information into bite-sized chunks, bullets help readers quickly scan and absorb the content. Remember to keep each bullet item brief and focused to maintain clarity and readability. The use of bullets not only improves comprehension but also adds visual appeal to your text, making it more engaging for your audience.

### Numbered Lists: Guiding Sequential Processes

Numbered lists are ideal when you need to guide readers through a sequential process or highlight a specific order or hierarchy. They provide a clear path for readers to follow, ensuring that information is presented in a logical and structured manner. Numbered lists can be particularly useful for step-by-step instructions, outlining project timelines, or summarizing a series of key actions. When using numbered lists, make sure to use consistent numbering and keep the text within each item concise and actionable. This format enables readers to navigate through the content effortlessly, promoting better understanding and retention.

## Subheadings: Organizing and Signposting Content

Subheadings serve as signposts that guide readers through your text, making it easier for them to navigate and comprehend your message. They break down your content into sections or topics, providing clear entry points and helping readers find specific information quickly. Craft informative and descriptive subheadings that accurately reflect the content they introduce. This not only aids readability but also enhances the overall structure and organization of your document. Well-placed subheadings allow readers to skim the text, locate relevant sections, and delve deeper into the areas of interest.

## Visual Appeal: Formatting for Engagement

In addition to improving readability, the use of bullets, numbered lists, and subheadings adds visual appeal to your content. Well-structured and visually appealing documents are more likely to capture and retain the reader's attention. The visual breaks created by bullets and numbered lists provide breathing space within the text, preventing it from appearing overwhelming or monotonous. Meanwhile, subheadings help create a sense of hierarchy, making the text more scannable and inviting. By formatting your content with these tools, you create an aesthetically pleasing and engaging reading experience.

## Striking the Right Balance: Avoid Overuse and Clutter

While bullets, numbered lists, and subheadings are powerful tools, it's important to strike the right balance and avoid overusing them. Too many bullet points or subheadings can overwhelm the reader and dilute the impact of your message. Use these formatting elements selectively, focusing on the most critical information or the most significant sections. Keep your content concise, ensuring that each bullet point or subheading adds value and relevance to your overall message.

# Avoiding unnecessary repetition or rambling

Incoherence and unnecessary repetition can hinder effective message delivery, leading to confusion and disengagement. To ensure your business communication is engaging and impactful, it is crucial to eliminate repetition and maintain coherence throughout your content. We will explore effective strategies to streamline your communication, captivate your audience, and convey your message with precision and clarity.

## Plan and Organize Your Content:

Before diving into writing, invest time in planning and organizing your thoughts. Start by identifying the main points you wish to convey. Consider the logical flow and structure of your message, ensuring that each point naturally leads to the next. By having a well-thought-out plan, you lay the foundation for coherence and reduce the likelihood of repetition.

## Use Clear and Concise Language:

Choose your words carefully and use clear and concise language to convey your message effectively. Avoid verbosity and unnecessary embellishments that can dilute your message or lead to repetition. Be mindful of your sentence structure and aim for brevity without sacrificing clarity. By utilizing succinct and straightforward language, you enhance comprehension and maintain coherence.

## Embrace Synonyms and Variations:

Repetition often occurs when we use the same words or phrases repeatedly. To avoid this, employ synonyms and variations to express your ideas. A thesaurus can be a valuable tool to expand your vocabulary and find suitable alternatives. However, exercise caution to maintain the context and ensure that the substitutions align with your intended meaning. By incorporating synonyms and variations, you infuse freshness into your writing and prevent unnecessary repetition.

### Transition Smoothly Between Ideas:

To maintain coherence, it is vital to establish smooth transitions between ideas and paragraphs. Utilize transitional phrases and words such as "however," "furthermore," or "consequently" to guide your readers through the progression of your thoughts. These transitional elements connect concepts seamlessly, eliminating abrupt shifts and reducing the need for repetitive explanations. By employing effective transitions, you create a cohesive narrative that flows naturally.

### Edit Diligently:

Editing is a crucial step in eliminating repetition and incoherence. Once you have drafted your content, review it with a critical eye. Look for instances where you have reiterated the same information unnecessarily or where your thoughts may be disjointed. Trim down repetitive phrases or sentences and restructure paragraphs to ensure a coherent flow. By taking the time to edit diligently, you enhance the overall quality of your communication.

## Seek Feedback:

To gain a fresh perspective on your content, seek feedback from trusted colleagues or peers. Ask them to review your communication for coherence and repetition. External input can shed light on areas that may require improvement or highlight instances of unintentional repetition. By actively seeking feedback, you demonstrate your commitment to crafting polished and coherent messages.

# Using proper grammar, punctuation, and spelling to ensure clarity

In the realm of professional correspondence, clarity is king. By mastering the rules of grammar, harnessing the power of punctuation, and embracing impeccable spelling, you can captivate your audience, build credibility, and convey your message with utmost clarity. We will explore the importance of these language fundamentals and provide you with valuable insights to enhance your written communication prowess.

## Grammar: The Foundation of Coherence

Proper grammar serves as the backbone of clear and coherent communication. It provides the framework that enables your ideas to flow seamlessly. By understanding and adhering to grammatical rules, you can construct well-structured sentences and convey your message with precision. Pay attention to subject-verb agreement, proper tense usage, and sentence construction. Remember, effective grammar ensures that your thoughts are articulated accurately, eliminating confusion and enhancing readability.

## Punctuation: The Art of Pausing and Emphasizing

Punctuation marks act as signposts, guiding your readers through your message with clarity and emphasis. Each punctuation mark carries its purpose and function. Mastering their usage allows you to control the pace, tone, and meaning of your writing. From the humble comma to the mighty exclamation point, each mark plays a vital role in shaping your communication. Embrace punctuation to signal pauses, emphasize key points, and clarify the relationship between ideas. A well placed comma or a strategically positioned semicolon can transform your message from a mere collection of words to a compelling narrative.

### Spelling: The Key to Professionalism and Credibility

In the digital age, where spell checkers and auto-correct features abound, the importance of accurate spelling cannot be overstated. Proper spelling demonstrates attention to detail and professionalism. It instills confidence in your readers and enhances your credibility. Take the time to review and verify the spelling of words, especially those with multiple variations or uncommon spellings. Double-check names, technical terms, and industry-specific jargon. Remember, flawless spelling ensures that your message is easily understood and leaves a lasting positive impression.

### Utilize Language Resources:

While grammar, punctuation, and spelling may seem daunting at times, there are numerous resources available to support your mastery of these essential skills. Grammar books, style guides, and reputable online resources can be valuable companions on your journey to linguistic excellence. Embrace these resources as reference points to clarify any uncertainties and strengthen your grasp of language mechanics. By expanding your knowledge and familiarizing yourself with the intricacies of grammar, punctuation, and spelling, you equip yourself with the tools to communicate with clarity and authority.

### Proofread with Precision:

Before hitting the "send" button, make proofreading a non-negotiable step in your writing process. Proofreading allows you to catch any grammatical errors, punctuation inconsistencies, or spelling mistakes that may have slipped through the cracks. Read your text carefully, line by line, paying attention to every word and punctuation mark.

Consider reading your writing aloud, as this can help identify awkward sentence structures or misplaced punctuation. Remember, precision in proofreading leads to precision in your message.

# Chapter 3

# Understanding the Power of Effective Subject Lines

## Crafting subject lines that capture attention and convey the purpose of the mail

In today's fast-paced digital world, capturing the attention of your recipients is paramount. A well-crafted subject line serves as a gateway to your mail, enticing recipients to open and engage with your message. We will delve into the strategies and techniques that will empower you to create subject lines that grab attention, pique curiosity, and effectively convey the purpose of your mail. Get ready to unleash the power of compelling subject lines that leave a lasting impact!

### Be Concise and Clear:

In a world flooded with mails, brevity is key. Keep your subject lines concise, aiming for a length of around 6-8 words. Be clear and direct in your language, avoiding ambiguity or cryptic phrases. A well-crafted subject line should provide a snapshot of the mail's content and immediately communicate its purpose. Consider including keywords that are relevant to the topic or action required, ensuring that recipients can quickly discern the value of opening your mail.

### Spark Curiosity and Intrigue:

Humans are naturally curious beings, and leveraging that curiosity in your subject lines can significantly increase open rates. Spark intrigue by posing a thought-provoking question or hinting at valuable information or opportunities within the mail. Use language that evokes curiosity and makes recipients eager to uncover the contents of your message. However, strike a balance by providing enough information to set clear expectations without revealing everything upfront.

### Create a Sense of Urgency:

To instill a sense of urgency and encourage immediate action, consider incorporating time-sensitive language in your subject lines. Highlight limited-time offers, deadlines, or upcoming events to motivate recipients to prioritize your mail. Phrases like "Limited Time Only," "Act Now," or "Don't Miss Out" can create a sense of FOMO (fear of missing out) and prompt recipients to open your mail promptly.

### Personalize and Segment:

Tailoring subject lines to a specific audience can significantly improve engagement rates. Utilize personalization tokens to address recipients by name or include specific details relevant to their interests or previous interactions. Furthermore, segmenting your mail lists based on demographics, preferences, or behavior allows you to create subject lines that resonate with specific groups, increasing the likelihood of them opening your mails.

### Experiment with Emotion and Creativity:

Emotion and creativity are powerful tools when it comes to crafting subject lines that grab attention. Consider using emotive language that taps into recipients' emotions and appeals to their desires or pain points. Inject creativity by employing wordplay, alliteration, or humor, as long as it aligns with your brand voice and the context of your mail. A subject line that stands out from the crowd and evokes an emotional response is more likely to catch the recipient's eye.

### Test, Analyze, and Optimize:

Subject lines are not a one-size-fits-all solution. It's crucial to continuously test and analyze their performance to optimize your mail marketing efforts. A/B testing can provide valuable insights into what subject line strategies resonate best with your audience. Monitor open rates, click-through rates, and conversions to gauge the effectiveness of different approaches. Use these learnings to refine and enhance your subject lines over time.

# Using keywords to facilitate mail organization and searchability

We will explore the art of keyword mastery, empowering you to organize and search your mails with precision and efficiency. Get ready to unlock the full potential of your mail inbox!

## Choose Relevant and Descriptive Keywords:

When it comes to mail organization and search, the selection of relevant and descriptive keywords is crucial. Aim to identify keywords that accurately represent the content, purpose, or key details of your mails. Consider the key topics, names, projects, or events associated with each message and choose keywords that encapsulate these elements. By selecting the right keywords, you establish a solid foundation for effective mail management.

## Create Consistent Naming Conventions:

Consistency is key when it comes to organizing and searching mails using keywords. Establishing a clear and consistent naming convention for your mails can significantly streamline your process. Whether you opt for a standardized format that includes project names, dates, or specific categories, ensure that you apply the same convention across all your mails. This practice enables easy identification and retrieval of messages related to specific topics or projects.

## Utilize Folders, Labels, or Tags:

Folders, labels, or tags are invaluable tools for organizing and categorizing your mails. Use them in conjunction with keywords to create a robust system that facilitates efficient mail management. Assign specific folders, labels, or tags to different categories or projects and include relevant keywords within their names. This combination allows you to quickly locate and group mails based on specific criteria, further enhancing your organizational capabilities.

### Leverage Advanced Search Features:

Most mail clients offer advanced search features that can make the process of locating specific mails a breeze. Familiarize yourself with these features and take advantage of their capabilities. Utilize operators such as "AND," "OR," and "NOT" to refine your search queries and narrow down results. Combine keywords with other search criteria such as sender, date range, or attachment to pinpoint the exact mails you're looking for. Mastery of these advanced search techniques can save you significant time and effort.

### Maintain a Keyword Reference List:

To ensure consistency in your keyword usage, consider maintaining a keyword reference list. This list serves as a centralized resource that captures the keywords you commonly use for mail organization and search. Update and expand this list regularly as new topics or projects emerge. Having a reference list readily available allows you to quickly and accurately assign keywords to new mails and ensures continuity in your mail management strategy.

### Regularly Review and Refine:

As your mail volume grows and evolves, it's essential to regularly review and refine your keyword strategy. Take the time to assess the effectiveness of your chosen keywords and make adjustments as necessary. Consider feedback from your search experiences and incorporate any new keywords that emerge. A proactive approach to reviewing and refining your keyword usage ensures that your mail organization and search capabilities remain optimized over time.

# Avoiding generic or vague subject lines

In the realm of business letters, ambiguity, and vagueness have no place. A well-crafted business letter should convey a specific purpose, provide relevant details, and drive actionable outcomes. We will explore the strategies and techniques to steer clear of general or vague topics, enabling you to create business letters that are professional, engaging, and results-oriented. Get ready to transform your written communication and leave a lasting impression!

## Define Your Purpose and Objectives:

Before putting pen to paper or fingers to keyboard, clearly define the purpose and objectives of your business letter. Ask yourself, "What specific outcome do I want to achieve?" Be precise and focused in articulating your intention. Avoid general statements or topics that lack clarity. Whether it's requesting information, proposing a partnership, or addressing a specific concern, ensure that your letter revolves around a well-defined purpose.

## Provide Relevant Details and Specific Examples:

To avoid vagueness in your business letter, back up your statements with relevant details and specific examples. Generalizations can leave room for misinterpretation and confusion. Instead, provide concrete information, facts, and figures to support your message. Use specific examples to illustrate your points and demonstrate the significance of your topic. The more specific and detailed your letter is, the clearer your message will be to the recipient.

### Use Clear and Concise Language:

Avoid using vague or ambiguous language that can lead to miscommunication. Choose your words carefully and opt for clear and concise language. Be straightforward in conveying your ideas. Steer clear of excessive jargon or technical terms that may be unfamiliar to the recipient. Use plain language that is easily understood and ensures that your message is communicated effectively.

### Address Specific Concerns or Questions:

In business letters, it is important to address specific concerns or questions directly. Avoid skirting around the issue or providing vague answers. Instead, tackle each concern or question head-on, offering clear and comprehensive responses. Anticipate potential doubts or queries from the recipient and proactively address them in your letter. By doing so, you demonstrate attentiveness and professionalism, leaving no room for uncertainty.

### Call for Action:

To avoid a business letter being seen as vague or open-ended, always conclude with a clear call to action. Explicitly state what you expect from the recipient and provide a timeline if necessary. Whether it's requesting a response, scheduling a meeting, or proposing a next step, make it clear and actionable. By providing a specific call to action, you ensure that your letter has a purpose and creates a pathway for meaningful progress.

## Proofread for Clarity:

Once you have drafted your business letter, proofread it carefully to ensure clarity and coherence. Look for any instances of vagueness or ambiguity and revise accordingly. Check that your message flows logically, each paragraph supports the overall purpose, and there are no loose ends. Consider seeking a second pair of eyes to review your letter from an objective perspective. Clear and error-free writing enhances the impact of your message.

# Including urgency indicators when necessary

In certain situations, it becomes crucial to communicate a sense of urgency through business letters to motivate recipients to act swiftly and decisively. We will explore effective strategies for including urgency indicators in your business letters, ensuring that your message captures attention, ignites a sense of importance, and compels immediate action. Get ready to unlock the power of urgency and achieve your desired outcomes!

## Choose Compelling Language:

When incorporating urgency indicators in your business letter, the choice of language plays a vital role. Select powerful words and phrases that convey a sense of immediacy and importance. Use action verbs to stimulate a sense of urgency, such as "act now," "respond immediately," or "time-sensitive opportunity." Employ persuasive language that resonates with the recipient's emotions and emphasizes the significance of the matter at hand.

## Highlight Deadlines or Time Constraints:

To create a sense of urgency, clearly communicate any deadlines or time constraints associated with the request or action in your business letter. Specify a specific date or time by which a response or action is required. Make the deadline prominent in the letter, whether through bold formatting, underlining, or strategically placing it in a separate paragraph or section. By emphasizing the limited timeframe, you encourage recipients to prioritize their response or action.

### Reference Consequences or Benefits of Immediate Action:

Another effective way to include urgency indicators in your business letter is to outline the potential consequences or benefits of immediate action. Highlight the positive outcomes that can be achieved by acting promptly, such as securing an advantageous deal, capturing an opportunity before it expires, or resolving a critical issue before it escalates. Conversely, mention the negative repercussions of delayed action, such as missing out on a time-limited offer or incurring avoidable costs.

### Utilize Visual Cues:

In addition to compelling language, visual cues can also enhance the perception of urgency in your business letter. Consider using attention-grabbing icons, symbols, or graphics that represent urgency, such as exclamation marks, arrows, or countdown timers. Strategically place these visual cues near important information or calls to action to draw the recipient's eye and reinforce the sense of urgency.

### Provide Clear Instructions and Next Steps:

To ensure that urgency translates into action, provide clear instructions and outline the next steps in your business letter. Make it easy for the recipient to understand what is expected of them and how to proceed. Clearly state the required actions and provide any necessary contact information, forms, or documents. By removing ambiguity and providing a clear roadmap, you facilitate immediate action and minimize any potential barriers or hesitations.

### Follow up and Reinforce Urgency:

After sending your business letter, it's crucial to follow up and reinforce the sense of urgency. If a response or action is not received within the specified timeframe, send a polite reminder highlighting the urgency of the matter once again. Restate the deadlines or time constraints and emphasize the missed opportunity or potential consequences of further delay. This proactive approach encourages recipients to act promptly and demonstrates your commitment to timely outcomes.

# Writing subject lines that are truthful and align with the mail content

In a world inundated with countless messages, it is imperative to craft subject lines that are both truthful and relevant to the content of the mail. In this article, we will delve into the strategies and techniques for creating subject lines that intrigue recipients, accurately represent the mail's content, and foster genuine engagement. Prepare to embark on a journey of subject line mastery!

## Be Truthful and Transparent:

Honesty and transparency are the foundation of effective subject lines. Your subject line should align closely with the actual content of the mail. Avoid using clickbait tactics or misleading statements that entice recipients but fail to deliver the promised content. By being truthful and transparent, you establish trust and credibility, ensuring that recipients know what to expect when they open your mail.

## Highlight the Most Important Information:

To make your subject line truly relevant, highlight the most important information or key benefit that the mail offers. What is the core message or value proposition you want to convey? Capture the essence of your mail concisely and compellingly, emphasizing the key point that will resonate with recipients. This way, they immediately grasp the relevance and importance of your message.

## Keep it Concise and Engaging:

Subject lines should be concise and engaging, capturing attention and generating curiosity. Aim for brevity while ensuring that the subject line captures the essence of your message. Use attention-grabbing words, action verbs, or intriguing statements that pique the recipient's interest. Avoid long-winded or convoluted subject lines that may cause confusion or disinterest.

### Personalize When Possible:

Personalization is a powerful tool for enhancing the relevance of subject lines. Tailor your subject line to address the recipient directly or reference their specific needs or interests. Incorporate their name or relevant details that demonstrate a genuine understanding of their situation. Personalization helps establish a connection and makes the mail feel more relevant and tailored to the recipient's individual needs.

### Test and Refine:

Subject line effectiveness can vary based on various factors, including the target audience, industry, and specific goals. To ensure optimal results, conduct tests and refine your subject lines based on the data. Experiment with different approaches, such as varying the wording, length, or tone of your subject lines, and analyze the open rates and engagement metrics. Use the insights gained to continually optimize your subject lines for maximum impact.

### Avoid Overused Buzzwords or Clichés:

While it's essential to craft engaging subject lines, be cautious of overused buzzwords or clichés that may dilute the impact of your message. Instead, aim for fresh, unique, and authentic language that stands out from the crowd. Tailor your subject line to your specific audience, avoiding generic phrases that may blend in with countless other mails. Be creative and strive for originality.

# Chapter 4

# Mastering mail Etiquette and Netiquette

## Being mindful of mail etiquette standards

In the digital era, mail has become a primary means of communication, making it essential to adhere to mail etiquette standards. Mastering the art of professional mail communication not only enhances your brand but also cultivates productive relationships and fosters a positive work environment. We will explore the key principles of mail etiquette, empowering you to craft mails that exude professionalism, competence, and respect. Get ready to unlock the power of mail etiquette and elevate your communication game to new heights!

### Start with a Professional Salutation:

The journey to impeccable mail etiquette begins with a professional salutation. Use appropriate greetings such as "Dear [Recipient's Name]," followed by a comma. Avoid informal or overly familiar greetings, as they can undermine your professionalism. If you are unsure of the recipient's name or gender-neutral salutations, opt for a more generic but still polite greeting, such as "Hello" or "Greetings."

### Use Clear and Concise Language:

Clarity and conciseness are key components of effective mail communication. Express your thoughts clearly and succinctly, ensuring that your message is easily understood by the recipient. Avoid lengthy paragraphs or excessive use of technical jargon that may confuse or overwhelm the reader. Be mindful of the recipient's time and strive for brevity while conveying your message effectively.

### Maintain a Polite and Respectful Tone:

Professionalism is synonymous with politeness and respect. Maintain a courteous and respectful tone throughout your mail. Be mindful of your language, avoiding sarcasm, rudeness, or offensive remarks. Use phrases such as "please" and "thank you" to demonstrate your appreciation and courtesy. Remember, every interaction is an opportunity to build and nurture professional relationships.

### Respond Promptly and Respect Deadlines:

Timeliness is a hallmark of professionalism. Respond to mails on time, acknowledging receipt of the message and addressing any urgent matters promptly. If you require more time to provide a comprehensive response, acknowledge the mail and communicate an estimated timeframe for a detailed reply. Respect deadlines communicated by the sender, ensuring that you meet them or provide regular updates if there are any delays.

### Use Proper Grammar, Punctuation, and Spelling:

Maintaining impeccable language skills is essential in portraying professionalism. Use proper grammar, punctuation, and spelling to ensure clarity and coherence in your mail. Proofread your mails before sending them to catch any errors or typos. Consider using proofreading tools or seeking assistance from colleagues to ensure your mail is polished and error-free.

### Exercise Discretion with CC and Reply All:

When using the CC (carbon copy) and Reply All functions, exercise discretion. Include only those individuals who truly need to be informed or involved in the mail conversation. Avoid unnecessarily cluttering inboxes and overwhelming recipients with irrelevant messages. Ensure that your use of these functions aligns with the purpose and relevance of the mail thread.

### Sign Off Professionally:

Conclude your mail with a professional and appropriate sign-off. Use phrases such as "Sincerely," "Best regards," or "Yours faithfully," followed by your name and contact information. Avoid overly casual or unprofessional sign-offs that may undermine the tone you have established throughout the mail. A well-chosen sign-off leaves a lasting impression and reinforces your professional.

# Responding promptly to mails

I am acutely aware of the importance of prompt communication in today's fast-paced world. In the realm of mail correspondence, responding promptly is a key factor that can propel your success and build strong professional relationships. We will explore the strategies and benefits of responding to mails promptly, empowering you to harness the power of speed and elevate your professional endeavors. Get ready to embrace the thrill of prompt mail responses and unlock new levels of productivity and success!

### Prioritize mail Management:

Efficient mail management is the foundation of prompt responses. Start by setting aside dedicated time in your schedule to review and respond to mails. Treat your inbox as a priority and make it a daily habit to clear your mail backlog. Implement a system for categorizing mails based on urgency and importance, enabling you to focus on the most critical messages first.

### Acknowledge Receipt and Set Expectations:

When you receive an mail, acknowledge its receipt promptly. Send a brief reply expressing gratitude and confirming that you have received the message. This simple act demonstrates your professionalism and assures the sender that their mail has reached you. Set expectations by providing an estimated timeframe for a detailed response if you are unable to provide one immediately.

### Keep Responses Clear and Concise:

When crafting your response, strive for clarity and conciseness. Get straight to the point and address the sender's questions or concerns directly. Use bullet points or numbered lists to organize complex information, making it easier for the recipient to digest and respond to. Avoid rambling or excessive details that may hinder comprehension and unnecessarily lengthen the response time.

### Leverage Tools and Templates:

To streamline your mail responses, leverage the power of tools and templates. Use mail clients or productivity apps that offer features like canned responses or mail templates. These tools allow you to save time by pre-drafting commonly used responses and quickly customizing them to fit each specific situation. Templates ensure consistency while expediting your response time.

### Avoid Procrastination and Proactive Communication:

Procrastination can be a productivity killer. Resist the temptation to delay responding to mails. Aim for a proactive approach by addressing mails as soon as possible. If you require additional information or cannot provide a complete response at the moment, communicate your progress to the sender. Proactively managing expectations demonstrates professionalism and maintains open lines of communication.

### Embrace Mobile and Remote Access:

In today's mobile world, embracing the accessibility of mail on your mobile device or remote access platforms can significantly enhance your response time. Utilize mobile mail applications or remote desktop tools to stay connected and respond to mails even when away from your workstation. Embracing these technologies empowers you to provide timely responses regardless of your location.

Responding to mails promptly is a hallmark of professionalism and a catalyst for success. By prioritizing mail management, acknowledging receipt, keeping responses clear and concise, leveraging tools and templates, prioritizing urgent and important mails, avoiding procrastination, and embracing mobile and remote access, you can unleash the power of prompt mail responses. Embrace the speed of success and witness how your promptness enhances your productivity, builds strong professional relationships, and propels you toward achieving your goals. The thrill of prompt mail responses awaits you—embrace it and seize the opportunities that come your way!

# Using appropriate greetings and sign-offs based on the recipient's level of familiarity

We will explore the art of selecting the right salutation and signature, enabling you to craft business letters that leave a lasting impression. Get ready to embark on a journey of salutatory excellence and elevate your communication prowess to new heights!

## Formal Salutations and Signatures for Unknown Recipients:

When addressing an unknown recipient, it is crucial to maintain a formal and respectful tone. Begin your letter with a salutation such as "Dear Sir or Madam" or "To whom it may concern." These greetings ensure politeness and professionalism, even in the absence of a specific name. Similarly, conclude your letter with a formal signature such as "Yours faithfully" or "Sincerely." These signatures convey respect and maintain a level of formality.

## Professional Salutations and Signatures for Acquaintances:

When writing to someone you have interacted with before or have a professional relationship with, it is appropriate to use a more personalized salutation and signature. Begin your letter with a salutation such as "Dear [Recipient's Last Name]" or "Hello [Recipient's First Name]." These greetings strike a balance between professionalism and familiarity. Conclude your letter with a professional yet warm signature such as "Kind regards" or "Best regards."

These signatures maintain professionalism while acknowledging the existing rapport.

## Informal Salutations and Signatures for Close Colleagues or Clients:

For individuals with whom you share a close working relationship or have a more informal rapport, you can opt for less formal salutations and signatures. Begin your letter with a salutation such as "Hi [Recipient's First Name]" or "Hello [Recipient's First Name]." These greetings reflect a level of informality while still maintaining professionalism. Conclude your letter with a casual yet respectful signature such as "Warm wishes" or "Cheers." These signatures strike a balance between professionalism and personal connection.

## Tailoring Salutations and Signatures to Cultural Norms:

In today's globalized business landscape, it is crucial to consider cultural norms when selecting salutations and signatures. Research and respect the cultural practices and customs of the recipient's country or organization. In some cultures, formal salutations and signatures are highly valued, while in others, a more informal approach may be preferred. Adapting to cultural norms demonstrates cultural sensitivity and fosters positive cross-cultural communication.

## Consider the Context and Purpose of the Letter:

The context and purpose of your letter should also guide your choice of salutation and signature. For official or legal correspondence, it is best to maintain a formal tone throughout. On the other hand, for informal or social letters within a professional context, a more relaxed salutation and signature may be appropriate. Tailor your choice to align with the letter's intent, ensuring consistency and appropriateness.

# Citing sources and providing necessary context when forwarding or replying to mails

When forwarding or replying to mails, it is crucial to provide sources and contextual details that support your statements and enhance understanding. We will explore the art of citing sources and providing necessary context, empowering you to engage in mail correspondence that is not only professional and competent but also informative and engaging. Get ready to unleash the power of well-supported communication!

## Citing Sources: Elevating Credibility and Accuracy

When forwarding or replying to mails, especially when sharing information or making claims, it is vital to cite your sources. By providing references or links to credible sources, you enhance the credibility and accuracy of your statements. This practice showcases your professionalism and commitment to reliable information. Ensure that your sources are reputable, up-to-date, and relevant to the topic at hand, reinforcing the validity of your claims.

## Providing Necessary Context: Enhancing Understanding and Clarity

Context is key to effective communication. When forwarding or replying to mails, take the time to provide the necessary context to ensure a comprehensive understanding of the message. Clearly explain the background information, relevant details, and any previous conversations or decisions that may be pertinent. By offering context, you enable the recipient to grasp the significance of the mail and respond in a more informed manner.

### Summarizing Key Points: Focusing Attention and Facilitating Response

To aid comprehension and facilitate a prompt response, summarize the key points of the mail clearly and concisely. Highlight the main ideas, action items, or questions that require attention. This summary acts as a quick reference for the recipient and ensures that the important aspects of the mail are not overlooked. By presenting information in a structured and organized manner, you enhance clarity and expedite the response process.

### Quoting Relevant Portions: Maintaining Clarity and Continuity

When replying to an mail, it is helpful to quote relevant portions of the original message to provide context and maintain continuity. Select and quote the specific sections that are relevant to your response, ensuring that the recipient can easily follow the conversation thread. By incorporating these quoted portions, you demonstrate attentiveness and prevent confusion or misinterpretation.

### Encouraging Further Research or Verification: Promoting Knowledge Exchange

In cases where additional information or verification may be required, encourage the recipient to conduct further research or seek additional sources independently. This promotes knowledge exchange and empowers the recipient to verify the information provided.

## Avoiding excessive use of capitalization, exclamation marks, or emoticons

In the world of business, it is crucial to strike the right balance between enthusiasm. We will delve into the art of avoiding excessive use of capital letters, exclamation points, and emoticons in your business communication. Let's explore how to maintain a professional, competent, and engaging tone that captivates without overwhelming. Prepare to embark on a journey of balanced expression!

### Capital Letters: Amplifying without Overwhelming

While capital letters can be useful for emphasizing a point or drawing attention, their excessive use can convey a sense of shouting or aggression. To maintain a professional tone, reserve capital letters for proper nouns, acronyms, or specific terms that require emphasis. Use them sparingly and intentionally to highlight important information, ensuring clarity and impact without overwhelming the recipient.

### Exclamation Points: Emphasizing with Elegance

Exclamation points are excellent tools for conveying enthusiasm or adding emphasis, but they should be used judiciously in business communication. Avoid peppering your mails with excessive exclamation points, as they can come across as unprofessional or overly informal. Instead, use them selectively to convey genuine excitement, appreciation, or urgency. Let your words carry the weight, with exclamation points serving as tasteful accents to elevate the message.

### Emoticons: Striking the Right Tone

Emoticons, such as smiley faces or emojis, have gained popularity in casual digital conversations. However, in a professional setting, their usage should be approached with caution. While an occasional well-placed emoticon can add a touch of friendliness or convey a specific sentiment, excessive or inappropriate use can undermine your professionalism and dilute the impact of your message. Reserve emoticons for informal or friendly exchanges with colleagues who are receptive to such expressions.

### Tone and Word Choice: Conveying Emotion Effectively

Instead of relying solely on capital letters, exclamation points, or emoticons, focus on crafting well-worded sentences and thoughtful language choices to effectively convey your intended tone and emotion. Choose words that are precise, descriptive, and engaging, allowing your message to resonate with the recipient. A carefully crafted sentence can convey enthusiasm or urgency without the need for excessive punctuation or emoticons.

### Context and Relationship: Adapting to the Situation

Consider the context and the nature of your relationship with the recipient when deciding whether to use capital letters, exclamation points, or emoticons. A more formal or unfamiliar relationship may require a more restrained approach, while a closer working relationship may allow for a slightly more relaxed tone. Adapt your communication style to the situation, always prioritizing professionalism and maintaining appropriate boundaries.

# Chapter 5

# Enhancing Clarity through Formatting and Visual Elements

## Using proper formatting techniques

Proper formatting not only enhances the visual appeal of your correspondence but also improves readability and conveys a sense of competence and attention to detail. We will explore the art of using the right formatting techniques to elevate your business letters to new heights. Get ready to embark on a journey of formatting mastery that will captivate your recipients and leave a lasting impression!

### Clear and Consistent Structure: Guiding the Reader's Eye

Begin by structuring your business letter clearly and consistently. Start with a professional and concise introduction, followed by well-organized paragraphs in the body that present your main points or arguments. Finally, conclude with a strong and succinct closing statement. Use subheadings, bullet points, or numbered lists to break up the content and make it easier to navigate. A well-structured letter guides the reader's eye and ensures that your message is conveyed effectively.

## Professional Font and Typography: Enhancing Legibility and Visual Appeal

Choose a professional font that is easy to read, such as Arial, Times New Roman, or Calibri. Maintain a consistent font size throughout the letter, typically ranging from 10 to 12 points, to ensure legibility. Use bold or italic formatting sparingly to emphasize important points or headings. Additionally, pay attention to line spacing and paragraph indentation to create a visually pleasing and reader-friendly layout.

### Proper Alignment and Margins: Aesthetic Harmony

Align your text to the left for a clean and professional look. Leave equal margins on all sides of the page to provide a balanced appearance. Ensure that your letter is aligned uniformly, maintaining a sense of aesthetic harmony. Proper alignment and margins contribute to the overall visual appeal of your business letter and reflect your attention to detail.

### Use of Headers and Footers: Professional Branding

Consider incorporating headers and footers in your business letter to enhance its professionalism and reinforce your brand. Include your company name, logo, contact information, and page numbers in the header or footer section. This not only adds a professional touch but also ensures that the recipient can easily identify and refer back to your letter when needed.

### Attention to Grammar and Spelling: Polishing Your Message

In addition to visual formatting, don't overlook the importance of impeccable grammar and spelling. Proofread your letter carefully to eliminate any errors or typos. A letter with flawless grammar and spelling showcase your competence and professionalism, instilling confidence in the recipient.

## Consistent Tone and Style: Unifying Your Message

Maintain a consistent tone and style throughout your business letter to ensure coherence and professionalism. Use appropriate language that aligns with the purpose and audience of the letter. Avoid slang, jargon, or overly formal language unless it is necessary for a specific context. Consistency in tone and style creates a unified and professional message that resonates with the reader.

# Emphasizing important information through bold or italics

In a sea of words, it is crucial to highlight essential details and key messages that demand attention and resonate with the reader. We will explore the art of using bold and italics to enhance the impact and clarity of your business letters. Get ready to unlock the power of empathy and captivate your recipients with precision and style!

## Using Bold to Emphasize Key Points: Directing the Reader's Focus

Bold formatting is an invaluable tool for drawing attention to crucial information in your business letters. Whether it's a critical deadline, a central idea, or a key benefit, employing bold text ensures that these important points are instantly recognizable amidst the sea of text. However, exercise restraint and use bold selectively to avoid overwhelming the reader. Each bolded phrase should be meaningful and contribute to the overall clarity and impact of your message.

## Italics for Emphasizing Titles and Foreign Words: Adding a Touch of Elegance

Italics can be used to add a touch of elegance and distinction to your business letters. Italicize titles of books, articles, or reports to differentiate them from the surrounding text and give them prominence. Additionally, if you are using foreign words or phrases within your letter, italicizing them can indicate their unique nature and help them stand out. Italics serve as subtle yet effective visual cues that add sophistication to your communication.

## Striking a Balance: Avoiding Excessive Emphasis

While bold and italics are powerful tools for emphasis, it is important to strike a balance and avoid excessive use. Overusing these formatting techniques can dilute their impact and make your letter appear cluttered or unprofessional. Instead, reserve their usage for truly important information that needs to be lighted. By employing them strategically, you ensure that the emphasized text carries weight and captures the reader's attention without overwhelming them.

## Clarity and Readability: Consistency is Key

Maintaining consistency is crucial when using bold and italics in your business letters. Ensure that the formatting is uniform throughout the letter, creating a visually pleasing and professional appearance. Avoid switching between fonts or styles excessively, as this can disrupt the flow and readability of your message. Consistency not only enhances readability but also conveys a sense of competence.

# Including relevant attachments or hyperlinks

In today's digital landscape, the ability to provide additional resources and facilitate easy access to valuable content can make a significant difference in the effectiveness of your communication. We will explore the need to include appropriate attachments or hyperlinks in your business letters. Get ready to unlock the power of bridging the gap and take your correspondence to new heights of convenience and engagement!

## Attachments: Delivering Rich and Detailed Content

Attachments serve as a valuable tool for delivering rich and detailed content to your recipients. Whether it's a comprehensive report, a detailed proposal, or supporting documentation, attachments allow you to provide additional context and information that may be crucial for the reader's understanding. By including attachments, you demonstrate your commitment to delivering complete and thorough information, elevating the professionalism of your business letters.

## Hyperlinks: Seamlessly Connecting to Online Resources

In the digital age, hyperlinks play a pivotal role in seamlessly connecting your recipients to online resources. By incorporating relevant hyperlinks within your business letters, you provide direct access to web pages, articles, or documents that offer additional information or support your claims. Hyperlinks save the recipient's time and effort by eliminating the need for manual searches, resulting in a smoother and more efficient experience.

### Choosing the Right Format: Consideration for Accessibility

When deciding between attachments and hyperlinks, it is crucial to consider the accessibility of your recipients. While attachments provide direct access to specific files, they may require additional steps to open and view. Hyperlinks, on the other hand, offer instant access to online resources but rely on an internet connection. Strike a balance by considering the preferences and technical capabilities of your recipients, ensuring that your chosen format caters to their needs and convenience.

### Proper Labeling and Instructions: Guiding the Reader

To maximize the effectiveness of attachments and hyperlinks, provide clear labeling and instructions within your business letters. Indicate the name and format of any attached files, and mention the purpose or relevance of the attachments in the body of your letter. Similarly, when including hyperlinks, use descriptive text that indicates the destination or purpose of the link. By guiding the reader and setting expectations, you enhance their understanding and engagement with the additional resources.

### Ensuring Security and Privacy: A Trustworthy Approach

When including attachments or hyperlinks, it is vital to prioritize security and privacy. Ensure that any attachments are scanned for viruses or malware to protect both your recipients and your reputation. When linking to external websites, consider the credibility and trustworthiness of the sources to safeguard your recipients from potential risks. By taking these precautions, you establish yourself as a reliable and trustworthy communicator.

# Organizing content using paragraphs or bullet points

In the fast-paced world of business, where attention spans are fleeting and clarity is paramount, organizing your content using paragraphs or bullets can make a world of difference. We will explore the art of content organization in business letters, discovering how paragraphs and bullets can bring order and enhance the impact of your message. Get ready to embark on a journey from chaos to clarity!

## Power of Paragraphs: Structuring Your Thoughts

Paragraphs serve as the building blocks of your business letter, allowing you to structure your thoughts and ideas coherently. Each paragraph should focus on a specific point or topic, ensuring that your message flows smoothly and logically. Begin with a clear topic sentence that summarizes the main idea of the paragraph, followed by supporting sentences that provide details or examples. By utilizing paragraphs effectively, you create a sense of order and guide your readers through your letter effortlessly.

## Unleashing the Bullets: Concise and Impactful

Bullets, on the other hand, offer a concise and impactful way to present information in your business letters. They are particularly effective when listing items, benefits, or key points. Bulleted lists break down complex information into bite-sized chunks, making it easier for readers to absorb and comprehend. Use bullets sparingly and strategically to highlight essential information, ensuring that each bullet stands out as a valuable piece of information in its own right.

### Clarity is King: Choosing the Right Format

When deciding between paragraphs and bullets, the key consideration is clarity. Paragraphs are ideal for conveying detailed information or explaining complex concepts, allowing you to provide comprehensive explanations. On the other hand, bullets excel at presenting concise information, emphasizing key points, or making lists more scannable. Evaluate the content of your business letter and determine which format best suits your purpose and enhances the clarity of your message.

### Strike a Balance: Combining Paragraphs and Bullets

The most effective business letters strike a balance between paragraphs and bullets, leveraging the strengths of both formats. Use paragraphs to provide context, background information, or detailed explanations, ensuring that your message is conveyed with depth and precision. Integrate bulleted lists to highlight key takeaways, benefits, or action points, capturing the attention of your readers and facilitating easy comprehension. The combination of paragraphs and bullets creates a dynamic and engaging reading experience.

### Visual Appeal: Formatting for Readability

In addition to organizing your content, pay attention to the visual appeal of your business letter. Use proper spacing and indentation to separate paragraphs, allowing readers to navigate through the text effortlessly. When using bullets, ensure consistent formattings, such as using the same bullet style and alignment. Consider the use of subheadings or bold text to create a visual hierarchy and guide the reader's attention. A well-formatted letter not only improves readability but also enhances the overall professionalism of your communication.

# Using numbered steps or instructions for clarity

We will explore how the strategic use of numbered steps can bring clarity, ensure comprehension, and streamline processes. Get ready to embark on a journey that will revolutionize the way you communicate instructions in your business letters!

## The Power of Numerical Sequence: Breaking It Down

Numbered steps offer a clear and concise way to break down complex instructions or processes. By assigning a number to each step, you provide a logical sequence that guides the reader through the required actions. This helps to eliminate confusion and ensures that the recipient can follow the instructions systematically. Whether it's a set of guidelines, a procedural outline, or a series of actions, numbered steps provide structure and enhance clarity.

## Highlighting Key Actions: Focus and Attention

When using numbered steps, each action or instruction stands out distinctly, capturing the reader's attention. By assigning a number to each step, you draw the reader's focus to the specific actions they need to take. This helps to prioritize important tasks, ensuring that the recipient understands the critical actions they should perform. Numbered steps serve as signposts, guiding the reader's attention and fostering a sense of direction.

## Concise and Scannable: Enhancing Readability

In the fast-paced business environment, concise and scannable information is essential. Numbered steps provide precisely that. Each step is presented as a brief and self-contained unit, making it easy for the reader to digest and comprehend the information quickly. The use of numbers also aids in scannability, allowing recipients to locate specific steps easily when referring back to the instructions. With numbered steps, you streamline the reading experience and ensure that your instructions are easily accessible.

## Breaking Complex Processes: Simplify and Clarify

Business letters often involve conveying complex processes or procedures. Numbered steps allow you to simplify and clarify these processes, making them more approachable for the reader. By breaking down complex tasks into smaller, manageable steps, you help the recipient grasp the overall process and understand their role in it. This promotes efficiency, reduces errors, and enhances collaboration, ultimately leading to smoother operations and better outcomes.

# Conclusion

In the realm of professional communication, proficient business mail writing is a cornerstone of success. By embracing these five unique guidelines, individuals can effectively convey their messages, exude professionalism, and foster fruitful relationships. Mastery of the art of business mail communication not only saves time but also enhances one's reputation as a competent and reliable communicator. Each mail sent presents an opportunity to leave a lasting positive impression and fortify professional connections. With these guidelines in hand, individuals can navigate the business landscape with confidence, wielding their mails as powerful tools for achievement.

# About the Author

Welcome, everyone. My name is Maksym Tanasov. My unparalleled imagination and deep understanding of the human condition have made me a literary luminary in the field of modern literature.

The origins of humble beginnings and experiences that have shaped my literary journey come from my childhood on the school bench in a remote small village, where my love of storytelling blossomed, to the influences of classic literature and the wonders of nature.

Take a journey through the evolution of writing style as you immerse yourself in my literary work, exploring the themes and motivations of my first debut.

Prepare to be captivated, inspired, and forever changed by the indelible mark of my prowess.

I look forward to continuing to share my work with you and hope that our paths will cross again soon.

# Acknowledgments
## Dear Readers,

I want to take a moment to express my sincere gratitude to each and every one of you for taking the time to read my book. As an author, there is no greater joy than knowing that your work has resonated with others and has made an impact on their lives.

Your support have been the driving force behind this book. Without your interest and enthusiasm, this project would not have been possible. Your feedback and reviews have been invaluable in shaping my writing and inspiring me to continue to grow as an author.

I am humbled by the overwhelming response that this book has received, and I am truly grateful for the opportunity to share my ideas and perspectives with you. I hope that this book has provided you with valuable insights, provoked thought-provoking discussions, and brought you joy and inspiration.

Once again, thank you for being a part of this journey with me. I look forward to continuing to share my writing with you, and I hope that our paths will cross again soon.